WHAT'S UP WITH MALCOLM?

THE REAL FAILURE OF ISLAM

A Quality Book™

WHAT'S UP WITH MALCOLM?

THE REAL FAILURE OF ISLAM

by

Haman Cross, Jr., and Donna E. Scott

with Eugene Seals, editor

A Quality Book™

Published by Moody Press, Chicago, and
The Spoken Word, Detroit, Michigan 48223

By arrangement with Quality Publishing Systems, Inc.,
Box 339635, Farmington Hills, Michigan 48333

1 3 5 7 9 10 8 6 4 2

Printed in the United States of America.

Contents

To You, With Love

I thought I knew what spiritual warfare was when I wrote *Wild Thing: Let's Talk About Sex.* However, the writing of this book and its companion *Have You Got Good Religion?* has been plagued with all sorts of assaults from the enemy of our souls. Dear reader, you would be surprised to hear of the enemy's attacks on me and on the other members of our team. But God gives grace to those who are within His will.

I am grateful for my loving wife, Roberta, who has encouraged me to share the message of Christ to a fallen world. Her support is indispensable to encourage a frail person such as myself to play my part in sharing the only message available for the upbuilding of all humanity.

Several other wonderful people deserve credit for helping to bring this book to you. Greg Thornton prodded me to set aside the time to develop the book and made insightful comments on the draft. Donna Scott and Eugene Seals helped me with so many details and are responsible for ensuring our high quality standards. Jabez Productions' creative perspective and Bonnie Gould's artistic gifts captured the essence of Malcolm's dilemma for our cover.

Paul Roebuck, former Muslim Five Percenter, was invaluable in providing hard-to-find research material.

And finally, you, the reader, can pass the message on to your friends and family. We don't need to see another mother's child succumb to the errors foisted on so many by the various chameleons called Allah.

Haman Cross, Jr.
August, 1993

Authors' Intent

It is not our intent to offend our Black Muslim brothers and sisters but:

- To share the truth as we see it
- To have readers act upon the truth as they hear it
- To stimulate readers to research these truths legitimately and experientially
- To respectfully compare the two most vocal religious alternatives presented to the African American community

The Night the Lights Went Out

Darkness – most of us fear the very thought. The word itself implies gloom, obscurity, mystery, dreariness, and even danger. When we were children, our mothers often turned on a night light to discourage the bogeyman who might be lurking in the shadows of our closet. Since then, we have leaned on one source of illumination or another to counter threats that might arise from darkness. Is this dependency? Quite the contrary. It is related to divine design.

The Bible says that "God is light, and in him is no darkness at all" (1 John 1:5). Yet, humankind still cringes from the hidden terror that night might bring. Pick up any newspaper, and you will see that our worst nightmares have become a reality. More than ever, monsters such as racism, crime, and poverty crouch behind every bush in a world that encourages victimization.

God never intended creation to be enveloped in darkness. In the first chapter of Genesis, one of His very first creative acts was to make a distinction by separating light from darkness. The light He called day; the darkness, night. After creating the heavens, earth, stars, galaxies, and so forth, God made another distinction. He created the sun and the moon – two great sources of light with two very separate domains. One rules the day; the other, the night. Whether the sun is the greater light is not the issue here. The point is that God never contemplated the universe being in darkness.

The moon is, as it were, our night light. It affects life and death. Winnifred B. Cutler is a scientist who has pioneered in carefully documenting the importance of lunar activity on the regulation of life. When people are not exposed to light, according to Cutler, they can become "out of sync" in a variety of ways. Such disruptions inhibit us from functioning at our best. Lunacy, she notes, is a real phenomenon. Consider the increase in suicides, homicides, hospital emergencies, and other crises at full moon.

What does this mean? Simply that things can become sane or insane depending on how we comprehend our dark situations. We can act a fool, howling at every trial and discouragement, or dance to the light of the moon. Because we have a free will, it is possible to harness our energies toward positive responses to poverty, unemployment, and racism. In fact, Darius Swan wrote in 1951:

> *In a world where suffering and hardship seem to be the dominant motif, the African American Christian's experience has better prepared him to make an outstanding contribution to the healing of the nations.*
>
> Destiny Video

The same holds true in 1993, more than forty years later. Consequently, Black Americans may be referred to as God's night light. Again, our particular struggles have uniquely equipped us to speak to the issues arising from moral, spiritual, economic, and racial darkness. While traditional Christianity's attempts to facilitate healing for both the oppressed and the oppressor have too often proven futile, the Black Christian's testimony is resplendent with solutions to regulate life again. However, when we ignore this call to be God's night light, the inevitable happens: a Malcolm X shows up.

This eloquent, yet angry, Black man carried the economic agonies and social hardships of an oppressed people to the doorstep of "Christianity." He pointedly stated our case against the church's complete failure to remove racism from its pulpits and its pews. He also galvanized thousands of African Americans to join his exodus from what he termed a "racist theology" toward the land of Al-Islam where he believed our "true and natural religion" could be found.

Though we empathize with the sufferings of this great Black leader, his "by any means necessary" dictum has left serious consequences. This book discusses how one man's being out of sync with his Creator eclipsed the light of the gospel in Black America by his repudiation of Jesus Christ.

Moreover, by examining his spiritual blindness, its causes and effects, we demonstrate that Malcolm is personally responsible for leading thousands of oppressed souls not only into the darkness of Islam, but also into the bosom of hell.

Join us, as we shed light upon what's *really* up with Malcolm X.

1

The Movement

This is the generation that will pass through the fire . . . . It is the generation under the gun . . . the tormented generation.

Billy Graham

When Malcolm Little was born in 1925, there wasn't a chicken in every pot, but there was pork. Meat was cheap, and home brew was strong. Duke Ellington was at the Cotton Club. Satchmo was at the Sunset. God was in heaven. Father Divine was in Harlem. The nation was giddy, and the Negro was in vogue (Bennett, 357).

Four years after Malcolm's birth, the stock market crashed with a sound heard not only on Wall Street, but on the streets of Black America as well. By 1937, approximately 26 percent of all Black males were unemployed; 65 percent turned to welfare in Georgia, while 85 percent staggered toward relief in Norfolk.

It was an era when grown men stood on street corners and sold their services. With few jobs in the North and fewer still in the South, many Blacks found solace in *Amazing Grace*. Others turned to Daddy Grace. The rest, decided to fall from grace, as did Malcolm Little later. The new deal Malcolm found was not in Franklin Delano Roosevelt's campaign promise of a fundamental new American utopia, but in a life of crime. For him, as for many other unemployed Blacks, the wounds from racism and poverty were just beginning to bleed.

For this confused young man, drugs, pimping, scamming, and stealing were the only gods that seemed to offer assistance during those dark days in America. "If blackness doesn't allow me to pursue the American dream, I'll find something that does," his deviant behavior seemed to imply. This all-too-common identity crisis soon landed Mr. Little in the Massachusetts penitentiary serving eight to ten for burglary. There, under the tutelage of his brothers Philbert and Reginald, he would exchange his gods of silver and gold for the gods of Islam. Although confined behind steel doors, his mind was nonetheless free to run rampant with indictments against White civilization.

For instance, Malcolm believed that his stiff penalty was more a result of associating with White women than justified by his petty theft conviction. Observers at his trial noted that burglaries of the kind Malcolm committed carried a maximum sentence of two years (Myers, 60). For Malcolm, it appeared that not much had changed since Gettysburg. A Black man could still be lynched for looking at a White woman.

Malcolm did not disagree that Blacks had begun to make inroads into the mainstream. Certainly the political genius of notables such as Robert Weaver, Ralph Bunche, and William Trent had been felt nationally and internationally. There was no question that Marion Anderson's critical acclaim boosted morale, as did the artistic achievements of Paul Robeson. But the triumph over centuries of racism would take more than intellectual and artistic excellence – more than Jesse Owens' one-man athletic *tour de force* at the Berlin Olympics.

For the average Black American, things were still going from bad to worse. They needed a country that offered more than dilapidated buildings, de facto segregation, and menial – though honest – service industry positions. Too long had Black Americans accepted the "White must be right" ethic. Somebody had to speak out against Klan violence, staggering unemployment, and segregated classrooms. The time was ripe for revolt. While James Baldwin, Ossie Davis, Ruby Dee, Leroi Jones (Imamu Amiri Baraka), and other intellectuals were calling for self-legitimization of the American Negro, Malcolm's mood – like the burgeoning jazz movement – became hot, hostile, and hard.

With Elijah Muhammad as his guide, Malcolm believed he had found the light. As a result, millions of Black souls were electrified, hypnotized, and "dehonkified" by the power of this one savvy, intelligent, albeit misinformed, Black man. The stage was set. During the next ten years, the races would reenact a centuries-old power struggle proving once again that, in the words of slain reporter Paul Guihard, "The Civil War had never ended" (Bennett, 385).

His Exodus. The movement for which Malcolm signed up and for which he later became chief point man, called for total separation of Blacks and Whites. His disdain for White America was demonstrated symbolically when he substituted the letter "X" (unknown) for his "slave name."

With some justification, Malcolm swallowed the rallying cry promoted by Wallace Fard and Elijah Muhammad that the enemy was the White man, that "blue-eyed devil." Of course, Wallace Fard – himself a

White man – was an unlikely Black leader if ever there was one. We will say more regarding this inconsistency later. In the contemporary volatile climate of American racism, their teachings were embraced readily and incorporated into the very fabric of Black life through its literature, music, politics, and theology (Bennett, 383).

Their basic tenet was that the Nation of Islam, also known as the Black Muslims, was the Black man's "true and natural religion." Christianity was of the devil, and the Black race was divine. God was given a color, Black, and an ultimatum: either He identify with the oppressed to the point that their experience becomes His; or He, too, is a racist. No in between. This kind of rhetoric fell on listening ears, and still does today. After centuries of unprecedented, inhumane oppression, Blacks felt like the children of Israel left alone in the wilderness during Moses' leave of absence. Malcolm and the millions of Blacks wandering with him wanted some answers. "Where is God? Why is He taking so long to deliver us? Who's going to bring us out of this oppression?"

Finally Malcolm came up with a solution. "Put all that you have – mind, body, and spirit – into the Nation of Islam, into the Quran, into Mecca. These be your gods. You will no longer be discriminated against." And yet, this false god corrupted the people.

His Reverse Discrimination. It appears that no one has the corner on racism. Evidence shows that the Nation of Islam is just as racist as any White supremacist group. Both promote the belief that their way of doing things is the only proper way. Whether it's pursuing the elusive American dream with a house in the suburbs, two children, and a dog, or facing the moon god of Mecca while dutifully praying five times a day, both have erected their own brands of sacred cows. Both believe in extermination and assimilation, citing each other as inhumane, and taking steps, however radical, to destroy the other. Both have their roots in fear and insecurity, the twin pillars of racism (Walter, 215-218).

Unfortunately, Malcolm had been blinded by the acts of "White America" so much that he was not able to rightly interpret the acts of the Nation of Islam. Nor could he see that Christianity is as Black as it is White. He could only focus on the hatred of lynch mobs, Jim Crow laws, and decades of discrimination. As he later concluded, the only place for a Black man was Mecca. We do not exist in this North American Eden – this White man's paradise – where Blacks should move to the rear, thank you.

His Search for Significance. Because of the limitations of space, we will only briefly examine the roles of Blacks in the Bible. For a more detailed exegesis, McCray's *The Black Presence in the Bible,* Felder's *Troubling Biblical Waters,* and Salley and Behm's *What Color is Your God?* are excellent study guides.

Nonetheless, the following discussion demonstrates that had Malcolm done his homework, he would have discovered that the Quran denies the value of our heritage whereas the Bible affirms it. According to Walter McCray and other noted scholars, our spiritual fathers did not hang out with Arab ancients near Mecca but with the descendants of Ham as they lived out their lives creatively all over the African-Asian world from the Tigris-Euphrates valley to the Nile and beyond.

It is accepted by both biblical and nonbiblical scholars that Noah's son Ham was the father of a line of explicitly Black African people who controlled not only Africa but also large parts of Asia, even settling as far away as North America (McCray, 56). Ham was the father of Cush, Egypt, Put, and Canaan. The ancient nation of Cush alone, often referred to as Ethiopia, covered large areas of Africa and Asia.

Even the descendants of Shem, from whom the Jews originated, have Black roots in their family tree (McCray, 158). A number of scholars go so far as to demonstrate that Abraham – the father of biblical Hebrew people – was Black (McCray, 122, 174-175).

The patriarch Joseph was influenced by the Black presence in his Egyptian community. Appointed agriculture minister under a Black Pharaoh, Joseph was given an African name, Zaephenathpaneh, and an African wife, Asenath, by whom he fathered two sons, Manasseh and Ephraim (Genesis 41:45, 50-52). As a result, two of the tribes of Israel had Black African ancestors.

During the great famine, when the entire continent of Asia went to Egypt for food, the Hebrew people relocated to Goshen, Egypt, an area influenced by the descendants of Ham. As a result, biblical religion received a significant African influence. Of the patriarchs, only Isaac did not spend significant time in Africa. In addition, numerous other biblical figures frequented southern Egypt and other areas populated by Black people. These included Melchizedek, Hagar, Rahab, Uriah, the Queen of Sheba, Abimilech son of Gideon, and Nimrod, to mention just a few notables (McCray, 116-117).

On the other hand, the Nation of Islam – supposedly the Black man's religion – is in actual fact a derivative of seventh-century pagan Arabia. Not only was Wallace Fard of Caucasian descent, but so was the author of the Quran, Prophet Mohammed himself. Robert Morey, a noted scholar who spent ten years studying Islam in the Library of Congress archives, located documentation to support Mohammed's claim that his pigmentation was that of a White man (*Hadith* 1:66).

Moreover, *Hadith* 1:662 and 9:256 go on to say that Prophet Mohammed took great pains to establish his White ethnicity and thereby dissociate himself from those whom he referred to disparagingly as "raisin heads and slaves."

In short, the man who brought the fabled Quran was Arab and anti-Black, whereas the man who delivered the Ten Commandments and wrote the first five books of the Old Testament had no problem associating with those of color and in bondage.

Moses, born in Egypt, adopted into the royal family, and instructed in the wisdom of the Egyptians, chose to identify with the Midianites, a Black people from whom he chose his African Cushite bride. Muslims, on the other hand, were forbidden to even dream of Black women.

Moses was also a military hero, conquering the kingdoms of the Amorites, Gilead, Bashan, and other nations (Deuteronomy 2:24-3:11). However, the only things Prophet Mohammed seemed to conquer were innocent teens. It is well documented that he fathered thirteen babies by various adolescent mothers, including one who was only nine years of age.

The point is this: If the eye is in darkness, the whole body is in darkness. Malcolm couldn't find his identity in the one true God of his African fathers, and thus he stumbled toward Islam's 360 pagan idols at the Kabah Temple. He embraced a transcendent god of the Quran, called Allah, and washed his hands of the personal God, Jehovah. He willingly took up the image of seventh-century Arabia while rejecting the God of the Bible.

He convinced millions of Blacks that their piece of the pie would come from the mythical Mr. Yacub (who supposedly used an early understanding of genetics to isolate carriers of defective White genes), the enigmatic Wallace Fard, or the self-aggrandizing Elijah Poole Muhammad. Quite to the contrary, our feast had, in fact, already been prepared by *Jehovah-Jireh* (the Lord, my provider) and was ready to be served.

His Evil Eye. At this point, many may object: "But look at all the good Malcolm did! You can't deny that." We affirm that there is indisputable truth in this position. Our point is that even as Malcolm indicted White Christianity for sowing racism, he himself sowed the very same seeds of hatred. Without question, Black Americans profited from Malcolm's calling attention to the inherent dignity and meaning of Black people. And yet there was much error mixed in with his truths. Malcolm was quite a man who, like so many others before and since, was not allowed to achieve his ultimate potential.

Let me illustrate: Suppose you have a glass that contains three-fourths dirty water. If you fill the remainder with clean water, is the result clean – or dirty? That was the point Jesus drove home in the parable of light. If the eye is bad, the whole body is in darkness.

The function of light is to show the body the way to turn. That's what the prophets of the Old Testament did. They afforded the listener some knowledge of Jesus Christ. No matter how dark the circumstances, if you look for the light, you will eventually get out.

Malcolm, however, first encouraged his followers to turn toward Mr. Muhammad. Then, when Malcolm began to see irreconcilable errors in the Nation of Islam, he pointed his entourage toward Mecca. Little did he realize that he was leading his people into a cultural religion that, from the seventh century to now, has maintained that forcing people into slavery, kidnapping women for one's harem, and raping them at will are just and proper spiritually sanctioned behaviors (Morey, 36).

Human culture says, "My way is right; yours is wrong." Islam's pagan Arab culture was no different from the Anglo-Saxon Christian culture that forced Malcolm's ancestors into slavery, kidnapped his great grandmother, and raped her at will, all the while misinterpreting the Bible to justify unprecedented acts of oppression.

His Tunnel Vision. Why could not brother Malcolm see the correlation? Simple. His eye was bad. He was in darkness. Thinking he had discovered his roots, he failed to see that even the very name *Islam* is an Arabic word associated with machismo, bravado, and heroism in battle. A seventh-century Arab was considered a hero for sneaking up behind someone and slitting his throat. That's not very different from the culture that assassinated Malcolm's own father. Even the term *assassin* is an Arabic word that describes Muslims who smoked hashish to whip themselves into a religious frenzy before killing their enemies. Islam moved to America with the Muslim sect known as the Assassins, who considered it their sacred duty to kill people – hardly a way to win friends and influence others (Morey, 39).

How could Malcolm miss the similarities between the Muslims and the KKK who had terrorized African Americans on nightly drunken raids? Again, the answer is simple: blindness – spiritual blindness. It would have been helpful for him to be aware of Paul's warning to the Corinthian church that the god of this world keeps people from the truth by blinding the mind of those who choose not to believe in the God of the Bible (2 Corinthians 4:4).

And yet, Satan was not content with just closing Malcolm's eyes to the God of the Bible. He also used Malcolm to mislead thousands of Black Americans as well. Capitalizing on the dissatisfaction of a growing segment of the Black population, beset with economic problems, haunted by the ghost of slavery past, limited social freedoms, and separate but unequal education, this blind guide led thousands of hurting people into a seventh-century Bedouin religion.

His false promises of freedom for the culturally and economically impoverished found receptivity in such diverse areas as South Central Los Angeles, Chicago's south side, and Detroit's Black Bottom. The proclamation of the divinity of the "Black Man" and the impending destruction of the "White Devil" was the best news they had heard since the Gettysburg Address. Particularly among low-income Blacks who needed an accounting for their obvious economic failure, these seeds of racial pride and self-dignity fell on responsive ground.

When people suffer, as we will further discuss in chapter 3, they become open to an answer, sometimes any answer, to assuage their pain. And so predictably along comes a David Koresh, a Jim Jones, or an Elijah Muhammad to take advantage of the weak and give them a false sense of hope.

Because Malcolm and Elijah Muhammad raised the Black man to new heights, the Nation of Islam became wealthy beyond their wildest dreams (Morey, 164). Their legacy is still alive today. But what exactly did these two leave behind? A trail of deception, fraud, reverse discrimination, greed, murder, and Louis Farrakhan. (We address the current Black Muslim movement in the companion book, *Have You Got Good Religion?* Here we concentrate on the earlier phases of the movement.)

Many, no doubt, may argue that most of the dirty work belonged to Elijah and that when brother Malcolm saw the light, he split. Even so, Malcolm is accountable for leading thousands, if not millions, of Blacks away from God and into the bosom of hell.

Is this possible? Can one man eclipse the light of an entire nation? Apparently so! The Bible tells an interesting story of King Manasseh. Incredibly wicked, he built high places for idol worship, astral worship, and Baal worship. He caused his own sons to pass through fire in ritual sacrifice. He indulged in astrology, familiar spirits, wizardry, enchantments, and every other evil under the sun. In short, he seduced an entire nation to do more evil than all the pagan nations troubling them.

God was so angry that he cut the people of Judah out of His will. In fact, God gave them over to the will of their enemies. Because of one man, sin entered their world, and death was the result. If the rap artist M. C. Hammer were to write Manasseh's epitaph, he would say, "You Can't Touch This."

But Malcolm came close. He left a legacy of hate, racism, and division because of his association with the Nation of Islam. Like Manasseh, the evil that Malcolm did has sown tares among the wheat. Before Malcolm – or before Mr. Muhammad, for that matter – Blacks had a heritage of believing God and the Bible. But since these two paraded as angels of light, Black America has never been the same. Because these men were not legitimate, their offspring – like the thirteen children Prophet Mohammed fathered – have come away empty handed. While Christians are regarded as the progeny of Abraham, nobody, not even orthodox Islam, claims *these* foundlings.

Yet upon closer inspection, you can see resemblances. Both Islam and the Nation of Islam have cultic influences. Both groups deny the Trinity and the deity of Christ. Furthermore, Islam's patriarch Prophet Mohammed had a strong attraction to young girls, and so did Elijah Muhammad.

Satanic verses (those containing contradictions to the Muslim faith) were used in both versions of their bibles with the gospels of Christ tacked on for added emphasis (Morey, 78, 169). Both religions are inconsistent, racist, and support terrorism (Morey, 20, 22, 166, 171, 173). Islam and the Nation of Islam favor the shedding of innocent blood (Morey, 39, 173). When you consider all that the two have in common, common parentage becomes apparent. No matter how loud the denial "This child is not mine," they've got their father's eyes: dark and evil. The evidence is overwhelming: Black Muslims are illegitimate children of orthodox Islam.

Parable of the Mustard Seed. Jesus talked about a mustard seed growing into the largest tree in a farmer's garden. Any botanist would tell you the abnormality of this phenomenon in that a tiny mustard seed can only produce a shrub. Yet, in the real world, mutant Ninja turtles – if you will – do exist. The growth of Islam and the Nation of Islam are not freak accidents. Both had experienced husbandmen who knew how to work a crop until it yielded one hundred fold. Unfortunately, the harvest was not for the kingdom of light but for the ruler of darkness.

Like God Almighty, the enemy's goal is to rule in the hearts of men. Unfortunately, most people cannot tell Satan's wicked messengers apart from the messengers of the God of the Bible. They are called prophets, saints, and even Allah incarnate. Although they fool the masses, God is not mocked. In fact, Jeremiah figured them out thousands of years ago: They promise *asalaam aleikum* (Arabic: peace, peace) when there is no peace (Jeremiah 6:14; 8:15).

Since the beginning of time, for everything legitimate, there has been something counterfeit. Malcolm X is an excellent case in point.

While a lot has been said about Malcolm's spiritual blindness and its influence on Black Americans, other questions remain. How did he get that way? What was the root cause? Was it his upbringing? His sufferings? Who is really to blame? These questions will be addressed in chapter 2.

2

The Man

I am not arguing that pain is not painful; pain hurts.

C. S. Lewis

"Why is this happening to me?" At one time or another, everyone has asked this question. It is the question Black freedmen asked when flogged by hatemongers in white sheets. It is the question the young ghetto mother asks when her eight-month-old baby succumbs to rat bites. It is the question six-year-old Malcolm Little asked when his father was run over by a trolley car. Whether sickness, death, financial devastation, a random car accident, or an act of nature, heartaches are shared by all who suffer.

Indeed, Job, probably the most intense example of human suffering, wondered the same thing. Once a wealthy man who lived by the book, in a short period of time he lost his house, his children, and his health. What made his pain and sorrow even more difficult was the apparent absenteeism of the God he had so piously served before. Worse yet, his suffering did not end there.

Three of his posse (running buddies) blamed Job for all his troubles. "It's your own fault," Eliphaz, the oldest, charged as Job sat homeless, scraping his boil-ridden flesh. "Besides," he added, "the innocent do not perish; the good are not destroyed" (Job 4:7, paraphrase).

Try using that reasoning on the young teenager raped by an alcoholic stepfather. Try using those words of comfort with a family whose son has lost a three-year battle with leukemia. Even if there were truth in these words, it would be, as Job said, "miserable comfort" in one's time of need. Isn't it strange how we naturally look for a scapegoat when calamity reaches someone's doorstep? *Something* must be the reason. *Someone,* probably the victim, must be the culprit.

For instance, in the ninth chapter of John, Jesus' inquiring followers wanted to know why a young boy had been stricken with blindness. "Who sinned," they inquired of the master Teacher, "the boy or his parents?" Who is responsible? No doubt young Malcolm Little wondered this very same thing throughout his childhood. "Who sinned? Who is to blame for all the troubles my family has seen?"

He Suffered. When Malcolm was four years old, his father, Earle Little, relocated the family to a farmhouse on the outskirts of Lansing, Michigan, despite hostile threats from White neighbors. A couple of weeks later, however, the Little's house was set ablaze by a group of locals angered by the illegal sale of property to Negroes. Malcolm and his six siblings watched helplessly as the fire department did precious little to keep their farmhouse from burning to the ground. Their next housewarming was little different. They were greeted with stones thrown by angry White neighbors who were trying to force the Little family to blacker pastures.

Things began to snowball out of control when six-year-old Malcolm was awakened yet another night to the high-pitched screams of his mother, Louise. In another cruel blow, young Malcolm's father had been crushed under the steel wheels of a trolley car. The timing of this tragedy could not have been worse. It was the beginning of the Great Depression, a time when Malcolm's brothers and sisters stood in food lines, along with other struggling Americans, desperate for a hot meal.

At school, he was ridiculed for his impoverished condition; and he held back the tears many a day while sipping leftover dandelion soup. The strain soon began to wear, not only on Malcolm, but on his mother as well. As a result, in January 1939, Louise Little was committed to a mental institution; and the seven Little children were parceled out to various state-run foster homes.

By the age of thirteen, Malcolm had been through a lot. He had seen his house burn down. He had been exposed to the violent death of his father. He had known extreme hunger. He had seen the slow breakdown of his mother. And he had seen his brothers and sisters placed in foster homes. Yet despite all this hardship, this afflicted young man determined to remain mentally tough. Remembering his mother's admonition to always study hard, Malcolm applied himself and excelled in school. Yet, even in this supposedly nurturing environment, he would not get a break.

No doubt believing he was doing young Malcolm a favor, his eighth grade teacher snuffed the last bit of light out of this tormented young thirteen-year-old's life. Asked about his future goals, the wide-eyed junior high schooler proudly announced, "I want to become a lawyer." One of the brightest students in his class, Malcolm had begun to prepare his mind for college by reading every book he could get his hands on. But nothing could prepare him for the all-too-typical blow his teacher would deliver to his dream:

> *We all like you, you know that. But you have to be realistic about being a nigger lawyer. That's not a realistic goal for a nigger. You need to think about something else you can be. You are good with your hands . . . . Why don't you plan on carpentry?*
>
> Myers, 37

This was the last straw. Malcolm would never be the same again. Having endured tragedy, violence, injustice, racism, rejection, alienation, and near starvation, this beleaguered young man could take no more. Enough was enough! Something had to be done about his constant mental anguish. R. Harvard, M.D., notes that, although mental pain is much less visible than physical pain, it is more common and harder to bear. It is easier to say, "My tooth is aching," than to admit, "My heart is broken." Yet, if the cause is faced, the conflict will strengthen and purify the character, and, in time, the pain will subside (Lewis, 156). Unfortunately, this would not be the case with young Malcolm Little. Unlike the following parable, he was tired of being strung out.

Parable of the Violin.

> *Years ago an old violin maker chose the wood for his instruments from the north side of the trees because, he said, this was the side that the fiercest storms beat on. At night when the storms came and the wind blew, the trees groaned under the lashing. But the violin maker did not feel sorry for them. "They are simply learning to be violins," he said.*
>
> Bragman

More Grace. Malcolm, however, never turned into a Stradivarius. Adversity's strains slowly made him feel like a broken-down fiddle. Before long, he started playing with the wrong crowd. First it was Shorty and the numbers racket. Then it was Reggie Little and the Nation of Islam. Next, he switched to Mr. Muhammad himself, Elijah Poole, the self-styled prophet of the Nation of Islam. None of these people could ease Malcolm's pain. Yet he continued to prefer the cacophony of strangers over the harmony of the Savior who offered unparalleled friendship, loyalty, and comfort.

After thirteen years of dandelion soup, family tragedy, and racial discrimination, Malcolm Little was sick of bowing down to suffering. "Who sinned?" Malcolm asked the Nation of Islam. "White folk," came the answer to this precocious, but undervalued, young Black man – one who in other times and circumstances, would have been, in Ossie Davis' words, "a shining, black prince."

According to the Nation of Islam, "White people are the cause of all the trouble you have seen. They are responsible for your father's being kicked under a trolley car. They are responsible for your family's being kicked from foster home to foster home. They are responsible for your mother's nervous breakdown." The Nation went on to maintain that the "White" God is responsible, too. "What kind of God would allow an impoverished, struggling family to be knocked down time and time again? What is the redeeming grace in watching your house burn to the ground on an icy winter night?"

And so for the first time, it all began to make sense! Now Malcolm began to articulate questions that had not occurred to him before. With convenient broad brush strokes, he could pin the blame on the "White devil" and his racist "White god."

"Where is the dignity in having your dreams of becoming a lawyer kicked to the curb? How am I supposed to stand if no one, including my favorite eighth grade teacher, will lend me a needed hand?" And yes, as Dr. Harvard notes, long, continuous pain develops either strength or resignation. Consider the following parable.

Parable of the Giraffe.

When a giraffe is born, the first thing the baby feels is its mother's tongue licking the birthing fluid off its newborn skin. After momma decides her offspring is all right, something strange takes place. WHAM! A swift kick in the rear end.

The baby is startled. After fifteen months of protective custody, is this what the real world is like? Your own mother turns on you? Imagine that! Unable to speak, he begins to moan. While pondering his misery, another swift kick floors him. Then another. And another.

Soon the frightened young ruminant wises up and minutes later wobbles to its feet. While teetering back and forth trying to maintain its balance, his mother kicks him down again. Again he manages to struggle up on all fours, and guess what? Another kick to the hind end. This is not fun!

Yet, with each painful kick, the young giraffe instinctively begins to get up faster and faster. Before long, he escapes his mother's seemingly abusive behavior. What an orientation to the real world!

Nonetheless if his mother would not teach him survival via this technique, the long-legged

creature would become easy prey for carni-
vores lurking in the wild. The mother knows
from experience that the only chance her in-
fant has for survival is his ability to quickly get
up on his feet. Otherwise, he is dead meat.

The God of the Bible knows that survival from the
wounds of sin, self-inflicted and other-inflicted, rests
on the ability to swiftly rise to one's feet. Malcolm
arose, but staggered toward the enemy's lair. He un-
wittingly mistook the God of the Bible for a foe who
was not for him but apparently against him. This
faulty belief led him to shun his Creator. From his
vantage point, Whites had constantly stomped his
rear end, both in the 'hood and at school. And, boy,
was it sore!

Like the baby giraffe, Malcolm had been given a
number of opportunities to figure out what was really
going on. His father had been struck down because of
his association with the Marcus Garvey movement,
aimed at uniting people of color. Nonetheless, Earle
Little kept getting up. And even though he lost his
home, he stood up to illegal housing laws. Earle Little
was an excellent role model of how to survive the
wounds of racial ignorance. Malcolm, however, for
all intents orphaned at thirteen, did not get the point.
Witnessing his family's disintegration made him un-
derstandably angry.

When you are an impoverished thirteen-year-old,
with only corn bread for dinner, God looks minus-
cule. It is only as you stretch out your neck above the
circumstances that things take on a different perspective – a heavenly aspect.

Pain's Origins. So where does all this suffering come
from? How did things get so out of hand? What makes
neighbors burn down an innocent family's farm
house? Why do young children have to eat dandelion

soup? Who is the cause of a young mother's becoming committed to a mental institution?

Sin – not skin, but sin – is the culprit. Sin is the cause of wars, racism, poverty, and pain. In the beginning, God created the heavens and the earth. After He had beautified His creation with trees, flowers, animals, and humankind, something terrible happened. Someone slithered into this perfect paradise and tainted it with hate, destroyed it with fear, and distorted it with a lie.

That someone was Lucifer, who was once the most beautiful angel in heaven, in charge of praising his Creator. And yet, this creature wanted more. Jealous of all the praise being given to God, Lucifer wanted to become the Creator and thus challenged God Almighty. After stirring up a third of the angels to revolt against God, Lucifer and his followers were expelled from heaven. Unfortunately for us, his rebellion did not stop there. He took his pride and bitterness and poisoned the Garden of Eden, up to that time the most idyllic home for human beings.

Beguiling Eve, the mother of humankind, he convinced her to rebel against God also by disregarding God's instructions concerning the Tree of the Knowledge of Good and Evil. By appealing to her pride, Satan enticed Eve to question God's love for her. As a result, Eve took matters into her own hands. With a single bite of some unnamed forbidden fruit, sin entered the world. And because misery loves company, Eve persuaded her husband, Adam, to join her in disobeying God. Although the Creator had given them wills that were free to choose between right and wrong, they chose to reject God's Word. From this first act of rebellion, the earth and humankind began to die. In fact, it was a three-faceted death:

- *Instant **spiritual** death*
- *Gradual **physical** death (as soon as we are born, we begin to die)*
- *Ultimate **eternal** death, except for Christ's saving grace* (Graham, 53)

From that day in the Garden until now, humankind began to reject God's Word and even God Himself. Instead of loving our neighbors, we burn them out. Instead of feeding the poor, we leave them to their dandelion soup. It is for these reasons and more that God came down to join us in our pain – to help us out of our misery.

Like Malcolm, Jesus was in danger from the time He was a child. He well understood the Littles' having to move from place to place. Jesus' family was forced to flee a murderous Roman king who did not want any Hebrew boys in the 'hood some 2,000 years ago. When Jesus became an adult, He encountered innumerable invitations to stand for more militant, less righteous causes, as well as countless plots to kill Him. And, finally, after a kangaroo court (much like the ones Klan members held for innocent Black men), a Jewish hate mob had Jesus crucified ("lynched," if you will) on Mount Calvary.

But three days later, Jesus overcame sin and death by rising from the grave. Because He was wounded for our transgression and bruised for our iniquities, He could identify with all the pain Malcolm experienced. He could show Malcolm the way from his grave circumstances, how to arise when the whole world is against you. God did not offer a Band-Aid for Malcolm's bleeding wounds but a life-giving blood transfusion in the person of Jesus Christ (Graham, 57). Nonetheless, Malcolm rejected the God of the Bible and His remedy for suffering. Instead, he turned to the nefarious Mr. Yacub for relief. Thinking Christianity was bad blood, Malcolm summarily dismissed the greatest story ever told.

Malcolm, it seems, was very much like the false prophet Barjesus. Paul refers to Barjesus as a child of the devil, full of subtlety and all mischief, an enemy of all that is right, who never ceased to pervert the ways of the Lord (Acts 13:6). Like Barjesus, Malcolm walked around in blindness as to the real cause of his pain – sin, not skin.

He Was a Soldier. Malcolm's incorrect response to adversity made him a real "trooper" for the Nation of Islam. Taking a quote from the Holy Bible, Malcolm informed Christianity that they were reaping what they had sown. Students of the era agree that Christianity ". . . failed to combat racism and so they reaped racism" (Salley and Behm, 61).

This mindset put more than the fear of God into White Americans. To add fuel to the fire, in 1959 Mike Wallace produced a riveting television documentary entitled "The Hate That Hate Produced." All across America, homes were bombarded with images of angry Black faces denouncing Whites. They were threatened by platoons of disciplined white-clad women – exotic and veiled – along with muscular young men training in the martial arts (Myers, 101).

Malcolm, the dutiful soldier for Mr. Muhammad, fielded questions concerning the Nation: *Did the Nation of Islam think all White people were the enemy? Were not the teachings of his mentor, the Honorable Elijah Muhammad, racist?* Malcolm's response was a cool rejection of those who had rejected him: "Our enemy is the white man. Oh yes, that devil is our enemy" (Myers, 106).

Before soldier boy came along, Black people had a heritage of believing God and the Bible. But once Malcolm arrived, thousands of angry Blacks wanted to annihilate the enemy of the people. Ossie Davis noted that Malcolm's favorite maneuvers included twisting the White devil's tail with regard to his failed race relations and making "Uncle Toms" (a misnomer for compromising and accomodating Blacks) ashamed. As a result, Malcolm was an unbearable nuisance to both Negroes and Whites.

For instance, Malcolm dismissed Martin Luther King's insistence that Blacks maintain their own humanity in the face of White oppression and that we are responsible to love our White brothers and sisters despite discrimination. Malcolm asserted that it was ridiculous for Black men to turn the other cheek when their women and children were being beaten and killed. Hostility is the only language, Malcolm said, that some folk understand (Myers, 121). He also had problems with King's Ghandi-style nonviolent strategy for achieving racial equality:

We are humbling ourselves, sitting in, and begging in, trying to unite with the slavemaster! ... The white man is telling you, you cannot live here, you cannot enter here, you cannot eat here, drink here, walk here, or ride here. You cannot play here, you cannot study here. Haven't we seen yet enough that he has no plan to unite with you?
Myers, 118-119

His mandate was, "To hell with White folks." He chided Black Americans to get off their knees and fight their own battles. Malcolm was willing to give his life for his freedom. As a good, committed soldier, he did not worry about the affairs of Mr. Muhammad because he was too busy doing the work the Nation of Islam had enlisted Minister Malcolm to do.

Malcolm advanced the notion that every White man had profited, directly or indirectly, from the

White man's collective foot being on the collective neck of Black Americans. Now it was time for reverse discrimination. Malcolm had no plans of fitting in, no intent to become the underdog again. According to him, "Revolution is bloody, revolution overturns and destroys everything that gets in its way" (Myers, 107).

That kind of talk was a royal pain to fearful White Americans, accustomed to being the dominant culture for 400 years with freedom to impose their injustices on Black Americans with impunity. The following parable illustrates the tremendous effect of Malcolm's irritating remarks on his White counterparts.

Parable of the Neck.

> *Imagine for a moment that your body parts call a summit meeting to determine who would be commander-in-chief. The brain says, "Since I already coordinate every function of the body I am the logical choice to give orders."*

> *The heart objects, saying, "Without my pumping blood throughout the body, no one would be able to function. Therefore, I should be running things." The eyes say, "Without us, no one would know where the body was going. We should be top gun."*

> *The mouth says, "I speak for the body. I should be in charge." One by one each member of the body gives its reason for being platoon leader. Finally, the neck speaks up, saying it should be boss.*

> *"You!" said the brain. "Why you? You don't do anything to begin with."*

"Yeah," said the heart. "We wouldn't even miss you if you weren't here. There is no reason for you to be the captain."

All of this makes the neck very angry. He becomes very tense. His muscles knot up, and he begins to exert excruciating pain. So intense is the pain that the brain cannot think. The eyes become blurry and cannot see well. And the heart has to work so hard that it becomes tired, skipping a beat every now and again. After a week of this, all the parts agree that the neck can be master.

Adapted from Elwin Collom,
First Baptist Church, Cohoma, Texas

He Was a Scourge. Malcolm was an immensely intelligent, skilled, committed Muslim who poured his heart into his cause. His biggest weapon was that he was a scourge to separatists, segregationists, and racists. His ascorbic remarks, bristling agitation, and scud-missile statements were aimed at scaring the devil out of White America. His battle hymn for Black Power made Malcolm the proverbial "thorn in the flesh" of traditional Christianity. In his words,

Christianity is the white man's religion. The Holy Bible in the white man's hands and his interpretation of it have been the single greatest ideological weapon for enslavement of millions of non-white human beings.

Salley and Behm, 60

Malcolm went on to say that, although Black people were supposed to be a part of the Christian church, "we live in a bitter world of rejection . . . being rejected by the White Christian church. In large numbers we became victims of drunkenness, drug addiction, reefer smoking . . . in a false, futile attempt to escape the reality and horror of the shameful condition that the slavemaster's Christian religion had placed us in" (Lincoln, 69-70).

What arose was a Black consciousness that totally rejected the White man's religion, values, attitudes, and assumptions. Christianity had become synonymous with oppression. A major result was that Black Americans – with the help of Malcolm X – redefined themselves. This redefinition did not seek to restructure Christianity so that it provided a religious expression for Blacks but totally rejected Christianity as a tool of oppression and as an ideology that fostered Black exclusion (Salley and Behm, 74).

According to journalist Louis Lomax, the main impact of Malcolm's indictment of Christianity has been the development of a Black theology and social protest that added impetus to the Black Muslim movement:

> *I have talked this over with scores of Negro clergymen, and almost to a man, they agree that Muhammad has deeply shaken the Negro Christian community. Muhammad's recital of how the Christian Church has failed the Negro – "By their fruits ye shall know them" – has sunk deeper into the hearts of the Negro masses than Negro clergymen will ever admit publicly.*
>
> Lomax, 188

Whereas most evangelicals mouthed pious irrelevancies and sanctimonious trivialities concerning racism, social injustice, and poverty, Malcolm – Elijah Muhammad's public servant – had a different message for the Black man in America. What was his message? Liberation! We will examine that message in chapter 3.

3

The Message

When I say by any means necessary, *I mean it with all of my heart and my mind and my soul. But a black man should give his life to be free, and he should also be willing to take the life of those who want to take his.*

Malcolm X

His Soapbox: Liberation. Malcolm realized that there existed a spiritual dimension to Black Americans, but he urged them to dissociate themselves from the White, blue-eyed Nordic Jesus who negated their humanity and their blackness while demanding that they whiten their souls to be saved (Salley and Behm, 72).

Yes, they should pursue freedom – but not at the price of the White "slavemaster's" wages of poverty, unemployment, and social injustice. There was no need to beg the White man for jobs and equality. Blacks should unite and help themselves. They should own what the master owned. They should enjoy the same freedoms that the master enjoyed. Instead of asking to be recognized as equals, they should *make* themselves equals (Muhammad, 62).

This platform was the grass roots of a truly distinctive and separate Black theology that was to be promoted by the religious leaders of the Nation of Islam (and subsequently by other fringe Christian leaders, such as Albert Cleage). Malcolm X, the Nation's charismatic preacher, delivered fiery sermons on the "White devil" with the lofty purpose of bringing holistic liberation to oppressed Black communities. According to his gospel, the Nation of Islam was able to speak to the social, economic, and political powerlessness of Black America.

This liberation, however, was based on a seventh-century pagan foundation. The very religion that he maintained would bring deliverance had, in fact, formed the vanguard in the slave trade. In the early crusades, it was the Muslims who wiped out African Christians in the name of Islam. Even the well-known abuses of Western slavery pale into insignificance when juxtaposed with the not-so-well publicized atrocities committed by Muslims against Black Africans. Even now in 1993, the *New Republic* and the *London Economist* report that chattel slavery continues in Mecca, where Black children are being sold for $15 a head.

Nonetheless, because of widespread disillusionment with White Christianity, Black liberation grew and flourished in the Black church (Ellis, 33, 84). For instance, Malcolm's contemporary, Albert Cleage, founder of Detroit's Shrine of the Black Madonna church, suggested that the "Black Sunday morning service was a waste of spirit." He, like many other self-styled Black liberationists, did not want Black Americans to forget brother Malcolm's teachings about the White enemy. "Instead of wasting time in emotionalism, churchgoers should be utilizing their power to confront the White enemy and destroy his system of oppression," he declared. The real power,

Cleage maintained, was in down-to-earth programs, not in frivolous Sunday morning hymn singing (Cone and Graynard, 337).

Cleage went on to say that "Blacks need not reject Christianity but only the White, honkified perversion of it that had been twisted and distorted by racists" (Salley and Behm, 75). Thus, Cleage's challenge to Blacks was to repudiate a White Christ. The Black Christian nationalist movement covenanted to rebuild the Black nation with power on earth. Pledging to fight injustice, oppression, and exploitation of all Black people, these disciples of the "Black Messiah, Jesus of Nazareth," declared that, according to Scripture, nothing was more sacred than the liberation of Black people (Cone and Graynard, 338). From seemingly inauspicious beginnings, Malcolm's measured doses of liberation theology eventually flooded Black theology. Because of his teachings, Black Americans are still trying to decide whether to advance to Christ or retreat to Mecca.

His Uncertain Sound. First Corinthians 14:8 notes that, if a trumpet gives "an uncertain sound," no one will prepare for battle. Hearing a bugle means nothing to a soldier unless a definite military call is played. Mere bugle notes are meaningless even when played by an official bugler such as Malcolm. It matters not if you start with the bugle of Elijah Poole then switch to the indiscernible sounds emanating from Prophet Mohammed's Quran. Random Arabic notes communicate zilch to Black Americans who are used to the language of hope contained in the Scriptures.

For 400 years, they had heard that the God of the Bible promises deliverance to all who trust in Christ. Now Malcolm was calling for trust in the Nation of Islam. Malcolm insisted that we did not need the White American Christ.

But whom would we follow in the name of Black liberation theology, given the plethora of voices clamoring for our allegiance? Would it be the enigmatic Wallace Fard, founder of the Nation of Islam, himself a White man? Would it be the self-styled messianic Elijah Poole, a Black man? Or would it be Prophet Mohammed, the deranged, immoral founder of Islam, a Mid-Eastern Caucasian? Further, how would he lead the fight in the battle against racism? By any means necessary? By following the Quran? According even to Muslim scholars, this Arabian holy book is too indistinct to give instructions or to have its instructions translated by mortal man (Morey, 118-119).

Indeed, language without meaning is pointless. The common purpose of a herald – be it bugle, Bible, or Quran – is to communicate understanding to those who hear it. Otherwise, it is useless. Malcolm, though eloquent, spoke confusing, reactionary words of hate to a people used to hearing about love. This malice blinded him to who the real enemy was. At first he led a charge against the White man. Next he said to advance toward Elijah Muhammad. Finally, he shouted, "Retreat to Mecca." Undoubtedly, many of the innocent people following him died in this "holy war" and went to an unholy hell.

As we discussed in chapter 2, Malcolm was without question, a model soldier. Always in a state of readiness, he never bucked authority. It was not until his commanding officer, Elijah Poole, had wiped out the lives of thirteen young women that Malcolm began to ask questions about the Nation of Islam. Even then he did not quit his unit. He merely switched to another tour of duty, the Kabah near Mecca. Donning Arabian fatigues, he went AWOL from the Nation of Islam and was subsequently shot as a traitor. This soldier's story ended in defeat because he fought on the wrong side from the beginning.

The book of Romans informs us that the God of the Bible has given us victory through Jesus Christ. What is the victory? Light over darkness, brotherhood over racism, love over hate, justice instead of injustice, and anointing in the midst of pain. Christ is still looking for a few good men and women who are willing to take up their cross and follow Him. Not Malcolm. Not Allah. Not Prophet Mohammed. But Jesus. The qualifications: death to self, to revenge, to hate, to idolatry, and to all other gods besides almighty and everlasting Jehovah, the God of the Bible. The good news is that you don't have to fight your battles or suffer alone. No weapon raised against you or your family shall stand.

Had soldier boy enlisted with Christ, He could have pulled down the strongholds of Klan violence, de facto segregation, and abject poverty. With Christ, Malcolm would have been invincible. Instead, his faulty belief that Allah could supply his need for identity, acceptance, and dignity caused him to lead thousands of equally deprived Black Americans backward toward the pit of seventh-century slavery.

Exodus 10:23 documents that even while all Egypt lay in spiritual darkness, there remained a light in the Israelite sector. Though surrounded by the spiritual darkness of slavery and racism, somehow their steadfast belief in the God of the Bible shone throughout that inhospitable land. This is the power of the gospel in the midst of pitch-black circumstances. Unfortunately, the gospel had been, and still is, hidden under a bushel basket by many mainstream evangelical Christians (Black and White), contributing to the fertile soil that allowed Malcolm to lead countless Black Americans into the wilderness of sin.

He Was Suckered. What happened? How did Malcolm's life, with such promise at age thirteen, end in such tragedy? Why was he shot down in his prime? The pain, anguish, and sorrow that he had experienced during the first decades of his troubled life were nothing compared to the wounds and betrayal he would receive from the Nation of Islam. It is a well-known fact that his body was riddled with bullets on February 21, 1965, in the Audubon Room. But it is not widely known that Malcolm's spirit had wasted away decades earlier. Like his spiritual advisor, Mr. Muhammad, he had been poisoned – although not by a woman, but by a snake. Remember the sound a rattlesnake makes before it strikes? That's what Malcolm heard when his father was killed, when he ate dandelion soup, when his mother was institutionalized, and when his family was split up.

The snake began to charm him. Although reluctant at first, Malcolm was gullible, allowing himself to be deceived. Apparently, he did not know how much he was seeking an answer to one of the great mysteries of the ages. Malcolm is a prime example of how hungry, hurting people are prime targets for deception. Not having his emotional, physical, and spiritual needs met created a growling in his stomach. Malcolm had already acquired a taste for dandelion consommé (soup). After thirteen years of starvation, he would swallow any morsel to fill his belly. It was at this point that the tempter snared him.

Preying on Malcolm's vulnerability, the tempter fed him a lie: "God is not for you. He is for the White man." John 10:10 refers to the enemy as the one who comes to kill, steal, and destroy. This potent lie destroyed the foundation that Malcolm's father, a Baptist minister, had laid. The only way to combat a lie is with the truth. That was Jesus' strategy at His showdown in the wilderness (Matthew 4). Because Malcolm had cast off God's Word, the Bible, as his focal point, he could not concentrate. Instead, he lost his balance and, eventually, his life.

The enemy had killed, stolen, and destroyed this confused young man's dreams for a family, a father, a home, and an education. Malcolm became a prime candidate for several helpings of "lie a la mode." His search for relief led to his seduction by the enemy's lies. He became ensnared in Satan's delusions.

He Was Sought. Why did this slithering snake pursue Malcolm? Why did he search him out? It was because Malcolm was not filled, and nature abhors a vacuum. Isaiah 55:2 admonishes the hungry soul to eat that which is good, that which will lead to fatness.

Again, for every proposal the God of the Bible has, the enemy has a counter offer. While Jesus offers you the Bread of Life (John 6), the enemy serves up the bread of deceit. "Yea, hath God said He is a God of the Black man as well as the White man?" Unfortunately, Malcolm gulped down every lie. His faulty belief system made him act out this distorted world view.

He Was Seduced. Because Malcolm was starved for the natural, legitimate cravings of the human heart – acceptance, family, significance, and dignity – he was vulnerable to seduction. While in jail, the false teachings of Wallace Fard and the Nation of Islam bewitched him. Of Elijah, Malcolm said,

> *He was the Messenger of Allah. When I was a foul, vicious convict, so evil that other convicts called me Satan, this man rescued me. He was the man who trained me, who treated me as if I were his own flesh and blood. He was the man who had given me wings to go places, to do things I otherwise never would have*

dreamed of. We walked with me caught up in a
whirlwind of emotions.

Myers, 38

Since Malcolm had disavowed the truth of the
Bible, he had no hope of breaking away from the
tempter's clutches. Slowly, but surely, he was enticed
and ultimately debauched by one prevaricator after
another.

It took some time before Malcolm discovered that
Elijah Poole was a greedy, covetous, opportunistic
womanizer. This polygamist lived in opulence while
Malcolm and other Muslims could scarcely pay their
rent. Elijah had two cars (a Cadillac and a Lincoln
Continental), $200 pin-striped suits (expensive for
those days), an eighteen-room mansion in the fash-
ionable integrated Hyde Park neighborhood of
Chicago, and thirteen concubines. Malcolm's life became circular. Again, he was the victim of bad deci-
sions. He had grown up with the dominant culture's
having the big houses, cars, and women while he
remained submissive. But Elijah's hanky-panky was
just too much. If you can't count on a self-proclaimed
messianic soul brother, whom can you trust? And so,
Malcolm's moorings came unglued.

He Was Snared. Disillusioned at the mind games
Elijah Poole Muhammad played on him, Malcolm
struggled to break free. When Elijah Muhammad
had Malcolm silenced because of remarks made
about the John F. Kennedy assassination, Malcolm
said, "I felt as though something in nature had
failed, like the sun or the moon." It really was his
own fault. Had he not turned his back on the truth,
he would have focused on the God of the Bible.
Instead, he eyeballed the lies of Prophet Mohammed.
And they were many. This so-called prophet was
raised in the moon god worshiping Quraysh tribe.
His mother was involved in the occult. Prophet

Mohammed himself was prone to epileptic fits that he would later label as miraculous visions (Morey, 71). Greedy, addicted to women, and illiterate, his claim to fame was allegedly being chosen to receive the visions recorded in the fabled Quran.

Seeing at last some of the shortcomings of the Nation of Islam, Malcolm longed to build a true Muslim organization with all the blessings of the Muslims of Africa and the Middle East. Though "authentic," it would nonetheless be structured on a Quran whose very foundation was on shaky ground, having gone through a variety of transformations over the years.

More Changes. Many of the accounts of Prophet Mohammed's call do not stand up to scrutiny. The Quran was conveniently changed from time to time to suit Prophet Mohammed's purposes. Whether they came by seizure or revelation, numerous amendments catered to *his* personal pleasure. When he wanted to marry his adopted son's wife, *he* received a revelation (Sura 33:36-38). When he wanted more wives or wanted to keep down bickering in his harem, *he* saw the light (Sura 33:28-34). When he did not want to be bothered with people, the spirit moved *him* to adopt visitation rights (Sura 29:62, 63; 33:53-58, 49:1-5; Morey, 145).

After finally seeing through Mr. Muhammad's masquerade, Malcolm allowed himself to be conned by yet another liar simply because he rejected the God of the Bible. He tried to run from the Nation of Islam and deprogram himself from Mr. Poole's illusions. But Prophet Mohammed's sleight of hand set him up for further exploitation.

In his sincere quest for truth, it is unfortunate that Malcolm was not aware of a growing consensus that the Quran is one big fake. It has no order. It is inconsistent. The language is confusing. The structure is weak and generally incoherent. A noted Muslim scholar asserts that the Quran is badly edited, illogical, and obtuse (Dashti, 28). A German scholar adds,

> *From a literary point of view the Quran has little merit. Declamation, repetition, puerility, a lack of logic and coherence strike the unprepared reader at every turn. It is humiliating to the human intellect to think this mediocre literature has been the subject of innumerable commentaries, and that millions are still wasting time absorbing it.*

> Reinach, 176

First Corinthians 14:33 insists that God is not the author of confusion but of peace. Unfortunately, Malcolm's blindness to the truth of the gospel led him into Prophet Mohammed's cavern of darkness. Thinking he had broken free of covetous men with licentious habits, he ingested even more lies. Hungry for truth and purity, he turned toward Mecca. His faulty belief that this was the true religion set him up for further deception.

Though not as well known in America, Mohammed was as much a crook as Elijah Poole. In the name of Allah, he plundered Jewish settlements near the Kabah. He had a faulty belief system that maintained that "greed was good." He even broke the very law he was supposed to uphold. The Quran said he could have but four wives. He had sixteen, including the wife of his adopted son. He bowed to the temple of Jerusalem first (for Jewish sympathy), then changed direction toward Mecca. It appears that Malcolm X wasn't the only person who had trouble making up his mind.

Had Malcolm not abandoned the truth, it would have made him a free man, liberated from the hook, line, and sinker of seduction. But he chose to serve a master who lied, cheated, and stole from him. His master was sin. Yes, he suffered. Yes, he was a loyal servant, a committed soldier. But he was also a sucker. He was bitten, poisoned time and again by the enemy's lies. His tale of woe is not unlike the following parable.

Parable of the Figs.

Once, an impoverished thirteen-year-old stole a box of figs and hid in his mother's tiny second-story flat to eat them. With only a small candle to chase the darkness, he fumbled to open the ill-gotten gains. He bit into the first fig and, to his dismay, tasted a worm. He bit into another and got the same result. Several figs later he realized that the whole box was crawling with worms.

Because his body ached with hunger, he had a decision to make. After several agonizing moments the young man blew out the candle. He had convinced himself that the darkness would take away the worms. By blowing out the candle he would not have to face his impending starvation.

Malcolm – by rejecting the gospel, the faith of his father, and the God of the Bible – did the same thing. His snubbing the Light of the World did not take away the worms of racism, poverty, manipulative whoremongers, or rejection. But, having gone without for thirteen years, Malcolm was ready to swallow anything.

The psalmist declared that, throughout his lifetime of seventy years, he had never seen the righteous forsaken or begging for bread (Psalm 37:25).

From experience he had learned that even in days of spiritual, emotional, and physical famine, those who trust in the God of the Bible shall be satisfied.

Had Malcolm tasted the Bread of Life, he would never have eaten at Elijah's table. Nor would he have thrown Prophet Mohammed's scraps to thousands of unsatisfied Black Americans. The light of the gospel would have exposed the worms of Islam.

But, just like the children of Israel, he was tricked, deceived, and suckered by some moldy bread (Joshua 9). Anxious to believe that there was some good in Islam, he was waylaid by the Quran, by Mr. Muhammad, by the enemy himself.

In Grand Rapids and Lansing, Michigan, his surname had been Little. In Detroit, they nicknamed him Red. In the Massachusetts penitentiary, he was dubbed X. In Mecca he became Malik El-Shabazz. But in heaven he is known as anathema (accursed).

What was the point of his life? What was the use? After all his preaching, teaching, and hemming and hawing, his was truly "a waste of spirit," to use Cleage's words. He never learned to tap into the real power source – the power of the gospel.

He was ashamed of his father's faith. He was ashamed of Christ. But Jesus would have saved him from a thousand devils: from years of dope peddling; from Mr. Muhammad's manipulations; from Prophet Mohammed's perversions; even from eternal damnation. Instead of being *suckered*, Christ's healing power would have *succored* him – would have helped him ease his pain, to have a moment of glory, to reach the winner's circle. Unfortunately, his story ended not unlike this modern-day parable.

Parable of the Horse Race.

There were two farmers who got together once a year to place a friendly wager. One year they might bet on baseball. The next year they might bet on football. The year after, they might bet on basketball. When 1965 rolled around, they got together to place their bets. This time they decided to bet on horses. Farmer Dale, tired of losing every year, figured out a surefire way to win.

He hired a jockey and upped the ante. Farmer Pete relied on lady luck. The race started, and – after a couple of lengths – the jockey riding Farmer Dale's filly was way ahead.

Moments later Farmer Pete's gelding caught up. As they were nearing the final turn, there was a collision. Both riders fell off their horses, but the seasoned jockey quickly got back in the saddle.

As he raced across the finish line Farmer Dale started jumping up and down, not in delight, but in frustration. Farmer Pete wondered why he was so disappointed, when he had finally won what he thought was a sucker bet.

"What's the problem?" he asked. "Didn't you get your money's worth?"

"No," fumed Farmer Dale. "The dumb jockey got on the wrong horse!"

The parable represents a way of looking at Malcolm's life. He placed his bet on the numbers as a young boy. Then he put all his hopes in the Nation of Islam. When he collided with Elijah, he switched horses.

As he raced toward the finish of his life, he did not realize he had mounted the wrong horse yet again. He never stopped to investigate, to look closely. The same could happen to anyone. If you've been saddled by the lies of Islam, there is still time to dismount. Malcolm – whose eye was evil, whose eye was in darkness – could not see that he was on the wrong horse. As his vision started to clear up, he was cut out of the race. You do not have to experience the same defeat. You can experience victory. You can make it to the winner's circle. The final chapter tells you how.

4

The Match Up

How long halt ye between two opinions?
1 Kings 18:21

Baal vs. God. In the eighteenth chapter of 1 Kings, the prophet Elijah initiates a showdown with the false prophets of Baal. Weary of his people's worshiping dead pagan idols instead of the living God of the Bible, he gathers together all the people on Mount Carmel for what many believe is going to be the ultimate sacrifice. In all, 400 prophets and thousands of Baal worshipers turn out for the big event.

To kick things off, Elijah says, "Let's have some fireworks. You take one bullock. I'll take the other. Let's dress them, cut them up, and put them on the altar. You call on your gods. I'll call on the Lord. Whoever answers by fire, let him be God. But I'll bet you 400 to 1 that your god is a punk!"

The prophets of Baal get fired up. They start out crying to their idol, confident that Baal will show up any minute and answer their prayers. Bringing fire down from heaven "ain't no thang" for Baal, they think. But, by lunch, nothing happens; and they become anxious for a reply.

So, for the next four to six hours, the prophets of Baal start jittin' and freak dancing up and down Mount Carmel. Elijah, bemused, articulates their worst nightmares by suggesting, "Why don't you scream a little louder? Either he is talking or running through the 'hood and can't hear."

The prophets of Baal take his advice, and the party gets wild. Cutting and slashing themselves, and falling on the ground, they beg Baal to bring fire down from heaven. Again, nothing happens, and after six hours of frantic madness, the party is over. Baal never shows up.

At that moment, Elijah steps to the dance floor. Taking his time, he repairs the broken down altar of wood, then fortifies it with stones. Next, he lays the bullock in pieces over the wood.

So that there will be no question as to how awesome his God is, Elijah drenches the altar with twelve barrels of water. At the time of the evening sacrifice, he calls on the name of the Lord, "Hear me, O Lord, hear me, that this people may know that You are the Lord God, and that You have turned their hearts back to You again" (18:37 NKJV). God answers, burning the sacrifice, the wood, and even the stones, then licking up the water in the trenches. The people fall on their faces and say, "The Lord, He is God" (18:39).

That was almost 3,000 years ago. But the same truths apply today. Whom do you represent in this story? Have you fallen on your face to Baal or to God? Many still have no idea who God really is. You think your situation has put you on death row, when you have really been seated in heavenly places. Some of you, if you are saved, are already standing in the winner's circle. But, because you choose to focus on your wounds and your bruises, you are not enjoying the victory God has promised through His Word.

Of course it's tough. Of course it's tight. You, like Malcolm Little, have had an extremely hard life. But God has brought you through. You are still alive. You can be the night light that shines in the darkness of pain, sorrow, and suffering. Revelation says they overcame by the blood of Christ and the word of their testimony (Revelation 12:11). Your life, your story, will help others who want to jump on the altar and cut themselves like the 400 prophets of Baal. Perhaps you, too, have considered giving up.

Your life is not that long. Last year is over. Yesterday is gone. You cannot afford to be overwhelmed, consumed with the battles you lost in the past. You must decide that since God has allowed you to go through these battles – racism, abuse, rejection – the very best way to become victorious is to give thanks unto the Lord for helping you make it through one more day. The very fact that you are still alive is a miracle. Consider this: More Americans were killed in the streets of Detroit or Washington, D.C., during the Persian Gulf War than in the war itself. You are blessed to be spared one more day. You are blessed to be able to read these words of comfort.

Young person, single person, married person, the God of the Bible did not keep you alive to serve a god that cannot hear you when you cry – a god that cannot help you when your teacher says that you won't amount to anything, that you will never be a lawyer – a god that cannot encourage you when your mother, husband, or friends say to give it up.

You are God's night light. Resolve to stop hiding under a bushel basket. You do not have to succumb to trials. Your purpose is to give light when things are dark. Your testimony can tell people how to have peace in the eye of a storm.

But it starts with a thankful heart. If yesterday was tough, give thanks. If last year was tough, give thanks. If your whole life was tough, give thanks. Quit crying about what the White man has and what you have not.

A pastor once said that many Blacks maintain they can't do this or that because of their pigmentation. My question is, How long is your skin going to be black? The rest of your life, I suppose. So you may as well give thanks among the heathen and sing praises to God. With Him nothing, even though you have black skin, shall be impossible.

You cannot go back and erase yesterday, last year, or your whole life for that matter. At this point, you are alive; you can hear; you can see; and you can breathe. In spite of how much you sinned and were sinned against, you survived. You may not realize it, but you are standing in the winner's circle. Therefore, before you take another breath to complain, "Woe is me; the world has done me wrong. Life is hard; somebody ought to pay," *give thanks.*

In the Bible, praise and thanks are associated with miracles. Malcolm, refusing to read the Bible and turning to the Quran, never figured this out. Before Elisha received the oil for the widow, he gave thanks (2 Kings 4:1-7). Before Jesus multiplied the loaves and the fishes, He gave thanks (Luke 9:16). The point is this: the miracles that are scheduled for you may be available tomorrow, this year, next year. However, you cannot receive them before you give thanks for yesterday, for last week.

Thanksgiving and *praise* come from the same root as *think.* Therefore, if we are more *thinkful* we will be more *thankful.* Philippians 4:8 is a list of things to think on: whatever is good, true, honest, just, lovely, worth giving praise for. You can, if you are a Christian, decide what you will think about.

Once you consider all the battles you have fought in your life, you can become thankful. You have already won the war. God already designed your victory. It may not appear – as it did not appear to Malcolm and many other oppressed people – that you have won. But don't look at the scoreboard; look at God. He is the Alpha and Omega, the beginning and the end. When the race is over, you will be in the winner's circle. God has never lost a battle. He did not lose on Mount Carmel against the 400 prophets of Baal, and He will not lose in your life.

You may be wondering at this point, *What do I really have to be thankful for? My boss is a racist. My husband is a jerk. I don't have a car. Everyone walks over me. I cannot see the forest for the trees.* The first thing you need to be thankful about is for who God is. For example, King David, after a long life of battles – of family, job, marriage, and financial problems – still decides that, in spite of his situation, he will thank the Lord (2 Samuel 22).

David made a choice. He chose the God of the Bible, not the God of the Quran. Many, like Malcolm and the followers of Islam, have never made that distinction. They should have. Why? Because they are not the same.

Make a choice. David did not say, I thank my higher power – or whoever is up there – or even the Man Upstairs, as God is often ignorantly referred to. Yet, even after what they have been through, many, like Malcolm, still do not understand. The reason the God of the Bible allows the changes, the oppression, the suffering in your life is so you can understand that what God does, no other god, including Allah, can do.

Right now, both mature people and young folk are crying, "Who will redeem us? Will it be Allah of the Quran or the God of the Bible?" God is asking you to be a night light in the darkness of police brutality, staggering unemployment, and perilous times – to testify how the God of the Scriptures delivers. There should be no question in oppressed peoples' minds as to who brings deliverance. As Baal's prophets learned, Allah cannot hear; he cannot deliver.

Malcolm whooped and hollered, cut himself, and by any means necessary cried out to his false god. But nothing happened. After his life ended, the evidence pointed to one thing: he was a false prophet. His god had no power, no fire. The god he believed in was not the God of the Scriptures. When King David fought against the Amorites and the Philistines the question was, as with Elijah on Mount Carmel, whose God was the "baddest," that is, whose God was the greatest.

Many feel that Islam should be tolerated because Muslims simply call god "Allah," that Allah is another name for God. Indeed, Malcolm, Fard, and Muhammad maintained that God's name is Allah. But that's heresy. That's false doctrine. If God be God, serve Him. If Allah be god, serve him. It's time for a showdown.

Allah and the God of the Bible are not one and the same. If they were, the concept of God in the Quran would coincide in all points with the concept of God found in the Bible. Let's examine ten differences between Allah of the Quran and the God of the Bible. We are grateful to Robert Morey for inspiring this comparative analysis.

God is knowable; Allah is not. The God of the Scriptures is knowable while the god of the Quran is unknowable. According to the Bible, God can be known. Jesus declares in John 17, "I came into the world so that you can know God."

After 400 years of oppression and bondage the children of Israel were led into the wilderness for the specific purpose of getting to know God. Daily they encountered hunger, thirst, enemies, fear. These problems were designed to prod the people to seek biblical solutions. Instead of being overwhelmed they were overshadowed.

As they ate manna from heaven, drank water from the rock, and defeated the kings of Sion and Og, they were given firsthand knowledge of God's provision, His deliverance, and His patience.

The Pentateuch was given as a written record of what they could expect from God. Exodus reveals who God is and who He is not. It reveals the character of God. And, it is regulatory in how He expected the people to behave. Through the Ten Commandments a distinction was made as to what God likes (obedience) and what He dislikes (rebellion). Throughout their wanderings, God's people were exposed to both His compassion and His righteous indignation.

Access to God is outlined in the twenty-six chapters of Leviticus. When do you approach Him? When do you stay away? What puts a smile on His face? What does not?

Obedience is the key to success in Deuteronomy and Numbers. In sickness and in health. In riches and poverty. In victory or defeat. No matter what the situation, the problem, the children of Israel knew what to expect from the God of the Bible. Not so with Allah. He is too transcendent. Too lofty. Too above it all to reveal himself to mortal man. You can't get to him, and he won't come to you.

This first distinction, knowable versus unknowable, should cause you to be thankful. When your mother abuses you, when you flunk that exam, when the policeman brutalizes you, the God of the Bible can be touched with your problems. You can find help in time of need (Hebrews 4:16). You should be grateful that you are not somewhere on your knees, pointing to the east, trying to serve and please a God you can never know.

The God of the Bible says, "I am the God who dwells among you, among your poverty, racism, discrimination, and heartache." John 1 tells us that He came among us. He pitched His tent with us and lived with our trials, our fears, and our worries. He walked with us, talked with us, and told us we belonged. The truth about God is that His name is not Allah. David stated, "Unto thee, thee who can be known, I will give thanks" (2 Samuel 22:50, paraphrased).

God is personal; Allah is not. The Bible tells us that God has a will. He has feelings – emotions. He was angry when the children of Israel constantly whined and complained (Numbers 13). He was pleased by the offering of Abel. He was delighted by Abraham's demonstration of faith (Genesis 22). He was miffed by Saul's partial obedience (1 Samuel 15).

Allah, on the other hand, is nonpersonal. Muslims claim that putting their god on a personal level would render him human. He would have to become personally involved with your triumphs and in your failures. But the God of the Bible is different. He *is* personal.

Let me explain. People around the country are impressed by many of the members of our church. "You mean to tell me that the president of a very influential national institute is a member of your church? That superstar basketball and baseball players attend your church? You can touch these people and talk to them? What is that like?" And yet, there are other members who may say, "Who are these people, I have never met them."

That's exactly what Muslims experience. "I know Allah is up there somewhere, but I don't really know him. You mean he came here, and I missed him?" Exactly. You will never catch up with this transcendent god. But the God of the Bible is personal. Jesus said, "I am the way, the truth, and the life" (John 14:6). No one can get to know the God of the Bible without knowing the Son on a personal level. Islam argues that you can never get to know god on a personal level. That is reason enough to thank God. He is so intimately acquainted with you, He even numbers the hairs on your scalp (Luke 12:7).

God is spiritual; Allah is not. Jesus says in John 4:24 that God is a spirit. For Muslims to say that Allah is a spirit would be blasphemous. That would demean Allah in their faulty belief system. One reason Jesus came was that everyone thought God was unapproachable – that you could not know Him personally. God sent Jesus to straighten out this errant thinking. God is a spirit.

What this means is that God can be everywhere at the same time. He is not limited to handling your crisis while I am destroyed on the other side of town. He is omnipresent.

God is Trinitarian; Allah is unitarian. This does not suggest that God is three gods as the Muslims would have you believe. God has revealed Himself as God the Father, God the Son, and God the Holy Spirit.

Understanding this principle is as simple as dealing with water. When liquefied, it is water. When frozen, it becomes ice. When heated, it becomes steam. Three distinctions, three separate functions, yet the substance remains the same. I may need water for a bath, ice for my tea, and vapor to clear my sinuses.

That is the same principle with God the Father, God the Son, and God the Holy Spirit. The three are one but have separate personhoods, separate identities that make them distinct. The Father provides for us what we need: food, clothing, shelter, discipline, correction. Everything that an earthly father does He does, only infinitely better. No earthly father is as protective, as loving, as kind, and as generous as our heavenly Father.

On the other hand, the Savior, Jesus Christ, does just that. He saves us from hell and from ourselves. He is our elder brother. He is the Son of God. He has lived where we are living.

The Holy Spirit is our guide. He comforts. He directs. He shows us through God's written Word, the Bible, what is right, what is not right, how to get right, and how to stay right (2 Timothy 3:16).

You get none of this through the Quran. You get none of this from Allah. He is only one, unitarian. Basically, you get more for your money with the God of the Bible.

God limits Himself; Allah does not. Titus 1:2 says that God cannot lie. Hebrews 6:18 states that God can never act in a way that is contrary to His divine nature. God says that He will limit Himself to His Word. He will limit Himself to His divine nature.

He won't act out of character. Since He is love, He will never do anything unloving. Because He is merciful, He will never act unmercifully.

Allah on the other hand, can do whatever he wants. If he decides to stop being just, he can do that. If he decides to stop being compassionate, he can kick you to the curb.

The God of the Bible does not want us to be surprised. He does not intend for us to live in limbo. He tells us what we can expect from Him. He limits Himself to His Word.

When the God of the Bible makes a promise, He cannot back down, regardless of how angry He may get with us. You can stand before Him and plead your case. For example, if you mess up and sin, you can tell God that His Word says, "though your sins be as scarlet, they shall be as white as snow" (Isaiah 1:18).

By His own Word, He has sworn that He will never forsake us or reject us. He does not change His mind. You will never see Him do anything outside of His Word. With Allah, who knows? Malcolm certainly did not.

God is trustworthy; Allah is not. The God of the Bible is consistent. He is not flaky. God has predicted what you can bank on. Deuteronomy 28:1-14 contains blessings you can expect if you are obedient. Verses 15-68 warn what will happen if you should rebel.

However, with the Quran, you have no way of knowing from one Sura to the next what to expect from Allah. What is commanded in one part of the Quran is often abrogated in another part (Morey, 112).

God is love; Allah is not. According to Muslims, Allah has no feelings. Yet Jesus Christ, our High

Priest, has been touched by our weakness, our pain, and our sufferings (Hebrews 4:15). You can have a personal relationship with the God of the universe. If it were not for His love, you might be burning in hell today.

While we were yet sinners, Jesus died for us (Romans 5:8). Christ did not say, "I'm gonna wait until you believe on me, then I'll die." In fact, when you were still shaking your fist at God, He had already paid for that act of rebellion. This is enigmatic to the human way of thinking.

God's love is a mystery in that most people would not jeopardize their life for a good person, much less for an irritant. Yet God so loved us that whoever will believe will have everlasting life (John 3:16). Malcolm did not have to go to hell. He chose to go there.

Even in Malcolm's rebellion, he could have turned to God, and it would have been finished. God would have wiped the slate clean. Malcolm would have experienced God's unconditional love. Nowhere in the Quran do you find such love. You find subjugation. You find revenge. You find by any means necessary. But you don't find unconditional love.

David says that he thanked the God of the Bible not because there was a gun to his head, but out of appreciation (Psalm 30). When David was a child, he read about the love of God. But it was after his sin with Bathsheba, when he took another man's life and wife, that he experienced the love of God (2 Samuel 12). It was then that God cleansed his spirit and restored the joy of David's salvation. It was after God put him back on the throne, after God forgave him, that David realized he was not worshiping Allah but Jehovah, the covenant-keeping God (2 Samuel 23:5). The God of David is the God of *hesed* (Hebrew: steadfast love), the love that says, "I don't care what you have done, I'm going to love you back to Me."

Even when you turn your back on Him, even when you are in the miry clay, God goes after you with unconditional love, stubborn love, love that won't quit, that won't wimp out.

When David's wife left him, when his boss rejected him, when his children abandoned him, when his kingdom pushed him aside, when his parents forgot about him, God Almighty, not Allah, chose him, set his feet on a rock, and established his goings. God will do the same for you today. He delivered Black Americans as a people when we had no power to repay Him. His name is God, not Allah. He is the essence of Love.

God allows us to go through trials, to experience darkness like the Jews in Egyptian bondage so that we can find out who He is. Many times we forget God, but He is ever mindful of us. Even though it's been tough and tight, we should give thanks to God for who He is. Namely, that He is not Allah. If He were, we would be in trouble. We would die in our sins.

That's exactly what happened to Malcolm. He perished in his sin and never became aquainted with the true God of the Bible. Instead, this false prophet went to his grave believing that Allah was God.

Incidentally, *Allah* was used as the personal name of a seventh-century Arabian moon god – a pagan deity. This Arabian moon god was said to be married to the sun goddess. Together they produced three daughters who were named the daughters of Allah: Al-Lat, Al-Uzza, and Manat (Morey, 50). The only thing this god seemed to love was the galaxies. With today's wounds, we need a god who is a tad more down to earth. Allah is not that person.

God is active; Allah is not. According to Muslims, Allah has always dealt through his prophet, angels, or the Quran. They cannot fathom God coming down and hip-hopping with His people. But the God of the Scriptures knew that Moses, John the Baptist, David, Elijah, and even Martin Luther King, Jr., could not save your soul. They all needed a sacrifice for themselves. The God of the Bible did not send a substitute, He came down himself. The God of the Bible has always been involved in our deliverance. Islam declares that Allah would never take on human flesh.

This particular difference between the God of the Bible and Allah can be further illustrated in the following story.

Once there was a little boy who received a train set for Christmas. He opened his present immediately and proceeded to run it around and around the track.

After a few minutes, the train derailed. The young boy became frustrated because he could not make the train wheels fit back into the track grooves.

His father, who had been silently watching, came over and offered his perspective. He assessed the situation and said to his son, "You will never get the wheels in the grooves working from above. You need to get down level to the track where you can see the problem and fit the train back onto the track."

God says the same thing. "If I remain in heaven, you will never be saved. Let Me come down here and eyeball you, and live with you thirty-three years so as to tell you that you can be set free. It is possible to live a life experiencing the presence of God."

The Allah of the Quran would never come down. Visit your house? Forget it. Live in your neighborhood? Wear you skin color? Go through what it is like to be single or married or a teenager? Allah would never do this, according to the Quran. But the Bible says that Jesus came. He was born in a lowly manger. He took on human flesh. He was rejected by His own.

Jesus went through everything you and I have experienced: shame, being misunderstood, lied about, spit upon, being hungry, being tempted. Yet He did not sin.

Jesus is eyeball to eyeball with us. He has been flesh of our flesh, bone of our bone. Therefore, He is the perfect sacrifice. Not only was Jesus active in history then, but He is also active now. When He ascended to the right hand of the Father in heaven, He sent the Holy Spirit to guide, teach, and empower us. Allah says, you're on your own.

God has positive attributes; Allah does not. Allah has ninety-nine attributes, all negative. *Hadith* 1 notes that Allah will not hear your prayers if you have bad breath. Allah will not forgive you if you pass gas. Allah is not love, Allah is not human. Allah is not personal (Hanagraph). But, the Scriptures reveal both the positive and negative attributes of God – what He is and what He is not.

Instead of following a god who is not even sensitive to natural human processes, you can serve a God who is familiar with our frailties and with our makeup (including halitosis) and still loves us. He is loving, merciful, and good. How do you know this? Last month, when you could have been fired, the merciful God of the Bible spared you. Last year, when your wife should have left you, you experienced the compassion of the Lord. When you should have been thrown in the streets, you experienced God's love. Moreover, the Bible tells us that God is not man that He should lie or take things back. What He says, He will do. What He promises, He will make good on (Numbers 23:19).

If you were to sit down and take inventory of your life, you would find situation after situation where you experienced God's love. Let the redeemed of the Lord say so!

God is grace; Allah is works. The Muslim, after he fasts, gives to the poor, chants, recites, goes to Mecca, and does all the other obligations of the Quran, is still unsure whether he will go to heaven. He simply hopes that perhaps Allah will be in a good mood the day this submissive, obedient, albeit deluded soul dies. There is no concept of grace.

But the God of the Scriptures says, "I am not going to give you what you deserve." All have sinned and fallen short, but God has given a free ticket to heaven through Jesus Christ (Romans 3:23: 6:23).

Because God is gracious, He is plenteous in mercy. If we confess the Lord Jesus and believe on Him in our hearts, we will be saved. This means that when we die, we have full assurance that Christ will tell us to enter in. But unconverted, mistaken Muslims will no doubt hear, "Depart from me, I never knew you." Not only do we have full assurance of a blissful eternity with the God of the Bible, Christians also have received the blessings of beginning their eternal life here and now. In response, they voluntarily renounce lying, stealing, substance abuse, gossip, and other sinful pursuits.

Because of the grace of God, all of your sins – past, present, and future – have been wiped away, forgiven. You can boldly, even after you have sinned, come to the throne of grace and have intimate communion with the God of the Bible. You can have confidence, even when everyone else believes that you do not belong at the throne, to approach God for help, for mercy.

That is why David praised God. Sure, there were those who felt he should not be king because he committed adultery. There were others who felt his lack of parenting skills disqualified him. The entire kingdom knew that one of his sons had raped his daughter and that another son had retaliated in murder. David had plenty of skeletons in his closet. He did not deserve to be king. He had literally blown it. But God's grace made him somebody. David knew how deep God's grace could go. There were sinful thoughts many did not even know about. The Psalms contain several statements of his desire to see his enemies killed. However, David went boldly to the throne of grace. And so can you. Today! You don't have to say like Muslims, "I hope he's in a good mood. I missed a couple of fasts, and I didn't make the trip to Mecca."

God is gracious. He will never change. He is the covenant-keeping God. He is not Allah. When the God of the Bible makes a promise, He keeps it. Difficulties and trials can teach us about the God of the Bible. Even if it is no more than that God is patient. We're still breathing, aren't we?

Of course life is difficult. You may catch it every day on your job. But you still have a job, don't you? Or if you do not have employment, the God of the Bible still feeds you. Why? Because He wants you to know that He is longsuffering, that He is dependable.

The reason the God of the Bible allows you to experience the dark night of the soul is so that you can set the record straight. Tell the truth – that it was He and not Allah who kept your marriage together. It was the God of the Bible and not Allah who kept you from flunking out of school, from cursing out your boss, from killing the man who raped you. It was the God of the Bible and not Allah who provided for you when you went bankrupt, who gave you a home after the bank foreclosed, who healed your disease when you should have contracted AIDS.

Even though it was the God of the Bible who came into the world, Malcolm could not comprehend His ways. Neither could Wallace Fard, nor Elijah Poole, nor Prophet Mohammed.

Many of you are standing in Malcolm's shoes. You have been wounded. You have been hurt. You cannot see why the God of the Bible allowed you to be fired, abused, discriminated against, or rejected. Yet you have a choice – as did Malcolm. You can remain in the dark about your situation – turn a blind eye to the God of the Bible. Or you can allow the light of His Word to correct your faulty vision – to make it clear that He has not abandoned you.

Malcolm never experienced Christ's saving grace. He never formed an accurate opinion about God's steadfast love and enduring mercy. Instead, he relied on false information and false ideologies. What is more, he kept getting on the wrong horse. His bad eyesight and evil eye blinded him to the truth. He died in bondage. He was never set free.

You do not have to end up that way. You can learn from Malcolm's mistakes. You can agree to accept the God of the Bible and reject the false gods of Malcolm X, Wallace Fard, and Elijah Poole. You can become God's night light, demonstrating His power over the darkness of racism, sexual abuse, substance abuse, police brutality, unemployment, and financial disaster. The choice is yours. How long will you waver between two opinions? If Allah be God, follow him. If God be God, follow Him.

For Further Study

Banks, William. *The Black Church in the U.S.* Chicago: Moody, 1972.

Bennett, Lerome. *A History of Black America.* Chicago: Johnson, 1987.

Brisbane, Robert. *Black Activism.* Valley Forge: Judson, 1974.

Cone, James, and William Graynard. *Black Theology: A Document History.* Maryknoll: Orbis, 1979.

Destiny Video. Atlanta: Destiny Movement, 1991.

Dashti, Ali. *23 Years: A Study of the Prophetic Career of Mohammed.* London, England: George Allen & Unwin, 1985.

Ellis, Carl. *Malcolm: The Man Behind the X.* Chattanooga, Tenn., and Union City, Georgia: Accord Publications and ICR Publications, 1993.

Felder, Cain. *Troubling Biblical Waters. Maryknoll: Orbis,* 1989.

Graham, Billy. *Hope for the Troubled Heart.* Dallas: Word, 1991

Hanagraph, Hank. Unpublished radio interview with Robert Morey. San Juan Capistrano: KKLA Radio, 1992.

Jones, Amos. *Paul's Message of Freedom: What Does it Mean to the Black Church?* Valley Forge: Judson, 1984.

Lewis, Bernard. *Race and Color in Islam*. New York: Octagon, 1979.

Lewis, C. S. *The Problem of Pain*. New York: Macmillan, 1962.

Lincoln, Eric. *The Black Muslims in America*. Boston: Beacon, 1961.

Lomax, Louis. *When the Word is Given*. New York: Signet, 1963.

Matthews, Victor H. *Manners and Customs in the Bible*. Peabody, Mass.: Hendrickson, 1988.

McCray, Walter. *The Black Presence in the Bible*. Chicago: Black Light Fellowship, 1990.

Muhammad, Elijah. *Message to the Black Man in America*. Newport News: United Brothers, 1965.

Muhammad, Elijah. *The Message to the Black Man in America*. Piladelphia: Hakims, 1965

Myers, Walter. *Malcolm X: By Any Means Necessary*. New York: Scholastic, 1993.

Mohler, James A. *The Sacrament of Suffering*. Notre Dame: Fides/Claretian, 1979.

Morey, Robert. *The Islamic Invasion*. Eugene, Oreg.: Harvest House, 1992.

Reinach, Salomon. *Orpheus: A History of Religion*. New York: Liveright, 1932.

Salley, Columbus, and Ronald Behm. *What Color is Your God?* Downers Grove: Intervarsity, 1970.

Steele, Shelby. *The Content of Our Character*. New York: Harper Perennial (Harper Collins), 1990.

Walter, J. *Sacred Cows*. Grand Rapids: Zondervan, 1979.

X, Malcolm, with Alex Haley. *Autobiography of Malcolm X*. New York: Grove, 1964.